I Love Ponies...

Pony Club

Sandy Ransford

C015035057

QED Publishing

Editor: Amanda Askew
Designer: Izzy Langridge

Copyright © QED Publishing 2011

First published in the UK in 2011 by
QED Publishing
A Quarto Group company
226 City Road
London EC1V 2TT

www.qed-publishing.co.uk

All rights reserved. No part of this publication may be reproduced, stored in a retrieval system, or transmitted in any form or by any means, electronic, mechanical, photocopying, recording, or otherwise, without the prior permission of the publisher, nor be otherwise circulated in any form of binding or cover other than that in which it is published and without a similar condition being imposed on the subsequent purchaser.

A catalogue record for this book is available from the British Library.

ISBN 978 1 84835 658 0

Printed in China

Website information is correct at time of going to press. The publishers cannot accept liability for the content of the Internet sites that you visit, nor for any information or links found on third-party websites.

Picture credits
(t=top, b=bottom, l=left, r=right, c=centre, fc=front cover)
All images are courtesy of Bob Langrish images unless stated below.
Alamay 14tr David L. Moore – Oahu, 14br ableimages, 18br Kumar Sriskandan
DK Images 7br Kit Houghton, 8 Dorling Kindersley, 10r Andy Crawford, 10l Kit Houghton, 11br Dorling Kindersley, 17tr Bob Langrish,
Shutterstock fc-r Groomee, fc-tl Lenkadan, 19tl cynoclub

Words in **bold** are explained in the Glossary on page 22.

Remember! Children must always wear appropriate clothing, including a riding hat, and follow safety guidelines when handling or riding horses and ponies.

Contents

Joining a riding club

Whether or not you have your own pony, you can have fun joining a riding club or a branch of The Pony Club. You will meet other children and their ponies, and learn a lot about riding and pony care.

The Pony Club
In Britain, The Pony Club is the junior section of the British Horse Society. There are Pony Club branches all over Britain. Each branch organizes rallies with competitions, an annual camp and other events. Other countries have their own versions of The Pony Club.

This young rider is wearing a Pony Club tie as part of her riding outfit.

Riding clubs often have their own premises, which will have a riding ring and fences for you to practise your jumping.

Going to meetings

Some branches of The Pony Club and some riding clubs hold meetings at riding schools, which means you can go along even if you don't have your own pony. They will let you handle and ride one of their ponies.

Indoor school

These riding club members are lucky to have the use of an indoor school for their lessons. This means that they can ride and do exercises in the saddle whatever the weather.

When you go to a meeting, an instructor will help you with your riding, and answer questions about pony care.

Going to meetings

You may be lucky enough to live near the meeting place of your club, and be able to ride there. If not, you will need transport for your pony.

Transport

Ponies can travel in either a **horsebox** or a **trailer**, which needs a powerful car to pull it. Sometimes you can share transport with a friend.

This large horsebox can carry several horses or ponies.

This trailer can be towed by a car.

Trailer travel

A pony can travel in a two-horse trailer, like this one, either with or without the central partition in place. Some trailers also have side ramps, so you can lead the pony out forwards – otherwise you have to back it down the ramp to unload it.

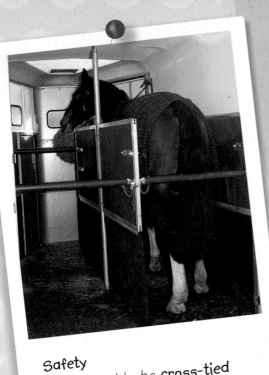

Safety
Ponies need to be **cross-tied** (tied on both sides) when they are travelling in a horsebox or trailer to stop them from trying to move about.

Into the trailer
When you lead a pony into a horsebox or trailer, walk confidently straight up the ramp.

This horse is wearing a travel rug, boots and a tail bandage.

Protective clothing
When a pony travels in a horsebox or trailer, it needs **travel boots** to protect its legs from knocks, and a tail bandage to prevent any rubbing. If you are not going far, it can travel with its **tack** on.

Learning more

When you go to meetings of The Pony Club or your riding club, you will learn a lot about ponies, such as how to keep your pony fit and healthy.

Top tip!

Learn the points of a horse so you know a forelock from a **fetlock**!

Points of a horse

It's important to know the correct names of the different parts of a pony's anatomy. Then you will know what people are talking about when they refer to, for example, its hock.

forelock

ear

crest

loins

withers

back

tail

cheek

nose

thigh

shoulder

chest

belly

knee

hoof

hock

fetlock

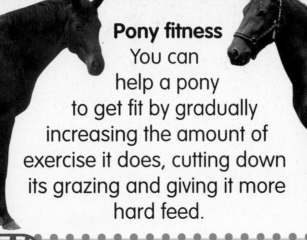

Pony fitness
You can help a pony to get fit by gradually increasing the amount of exercise it does, cutting down its grazing and giving it more hard feed.

fat, grass-fed pony

fit pony

How to lead a pony
Lead your pony on its left side, with your right hand near its head and your left hand at the end of the rope. Then, if needed, you can let go with your right hand and bring the pony round with your left hand.

Approaching a strange pony
Walk towards the pony's head from one side. Speak to it, let it sniff your closed fist, and pat it on the neck. That way the pony knows that you are a friend.

Improving your riding

Some of your riding club meetings will show you exercises to improve your riding and give you more confidence in the saddle. Some of these can be done while the horse is led on a long rein that is attached to a special headcollar. This is called **lungeing**.

On the lunge, without stirrups

Riding with your stirrups crossed over your saddle will help to improve your seat in the saddle and your balance. If you feel insecure, hold on to the front of the saddle.

On the lunge, without reins

Knotting your reins and riding without them will also improve your balance when riding. The person holding the lunge rein will control the pony.

Riding without stirrups in trot is very bumpy! You have to learn to sit really deeply in the saddle.

Exercises in the saddle

There are lots of exercises you can do while you are sitting on a pony as long as someone is holding it for you. The exercises will make you supple and give you more confidence.

Hold your arms out and twist round to each side from your waist.

Touching your toes

Lift your right hand up in the air then bend down to touch your left foot. Straighten up, then repeat the exercise with your left hand touching your right foot.

Lying back

Lie back until your head touches the pony's back. Try to sit up again without holding on to the saddle, but if you can't, then pull yourself up using the front of the saddle.

Working harder

As your riding improves, you will learn more advanced exercises, and also how to handle problem ponies.

Making your pony move

Some ponies don't want to go forwards. To encourage your pony, shorten the reins, squeeze hard with your legs, and say firmly, "Walk on". If it still doesn't move, you can use a stick just behind the girth (the strap under the horse's belly) to reinforce your leg aid.

Moving too quickly

Some ponies want to set off at great speed, especially when they canter. First of all, never lean forwards, as this will make the pony think you want it to go faster. Keep your reins short and sit down in the saddle. If possible, try to ride the pony round in a circle to slow it down, but don't turn it too fast or it could fall over.

Working as a pair

Riding round side by side with another pony is a good exercise in control. There are classes for riding in pairs at shows, and it's fun to do, though much more difficult than it looks. The ponies' heads should be level, and remember that when you turn, the pony on the outside has to move faster than the one on the inside.

Meet-up fact!
Ponies ridden side by side may want to race each other if they canter.

When riding as a pair, it's easier if the larger pony is on the outer side of the smaller one.

Pony Club camp

Every summer, branches of The Pony Club and some riding clubs go away to camp. It's a chance to have lots of fun with your friends and their ponies.

At the camp

You will probably sleep in a tent, and your pony will be turned out with the others in a field. You will have to look after your pony yourself, and also help with cooking meals and keeping the camp tidy.

These ponies have had their morning ride and are resting before a lesson in the school later on.

My Pony Club camp diary

7 a.m. I crawled out of my sleeping bag, got dressed and went out to feed the ponies. It's a bright, sunny day – hooray!

7.30 a.m. Our leader built a fire and fried eggs over it. We had a yummy breakfast.

8.30 a.m. After washing-up, we groomed and tacked up the ponies.

9 a.m. We set off on a long ride. Luckily, our camp was near the sea, so we rode along the beach. We tried riding in the shallow water, but some of the ponies didn't want to go in!

12.30 p.m. We returned to camp, brushed the ponies over and turned them out in the field.

1 p.m. Picnic time! We all had lunch on the grass.

2 p.m. After lunch, we went into the indoor school for a talk about pony care and feeding by one of The Pony Club officials. I had no idea there was so much to learn!

5 p.m. Dinnertime, with a cake for dessert. Then we cleaned the tack.

7 p.m. We checked the ponies one last time and then went back to our tents and got ready to go to sleep. It was supposed to be lights out at 8 p.m., but I was so tired, I was asleep long before that!

Having fun

You will have a great time away at camp, with nothing but ponies to think about. You will spend your whole day riding them and caring for them.

Group sessions
You may have group lessons with other riders in a field or an outdoor school. These may be lessons in basic riding, or more advanced skills, such as jumping.

Riding for a day
You may go out on a whole day's ride, taking a packed lunch with you. Your pony may wear a headcollar over its bridle, so you can remove its **bit** and allow it to graze at lunch time. You will also stop to let it drink when you are near water.

Aftercare

After riding, you will need to take water and food to your pony before you have your own meal. If it is put in a stable, it will also need hay.

Cleaning the tack

To make this task more fun, do it with your friends. First, clean off the grease and any mud with a damp sponge, then rub in saddle soap. Wet the soap, not the sponge, to avoid getting too much lather.

At the end of the day's riding you will need to clean the pony's tack (its saddle and bridle).

Top tip!

If you keep your tack clean and supple, it will last for many years.

Competitions

As well as having riding lessons, learning how to look after ponies and going on long hacks, your camp may hold competitions.

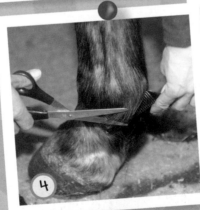

Best turned out pony

To win this competition, you will need to:

1. Groom your pony until its coat gleams.

2. Wash and dry its mane and tail.

3. Wash and dry its white socks.

4. Trim the long hair on its fetlocks.

5. Brush any mud off its hooves and oil them.

6. Clean and saddle-soap the tack.

Best turned out rider

You will need to look your cleanest and smartest to win!

Beginners' dressage

Your camp may have a **dressage** arena, and they may hold dressage competitions. Even if you're not very good at it, it's great practice for both you and your pony.

This pony is doing a **collected walk**. Ponies may wear bandages on their lower legs when they are working to support their tendons.

These pumpkins make an unusual jump, which some ponies may not like!

Jumping course

There will probably be a jumping course, either of show jumps with coloured poles or cross-country fences. Even if you don't compete, you can learn a lot by trying out all the different kinds of jump.

Team games

Your riding club or branch of the Pony Club may have a team that competes in gymkhana events, such as relay races. If you have a pony that can gallop and turn quickly, and you are good at jumping on and off, you may be able to join the team.

Old sock race
In this race, each competitor collects a rolled-up sock, gallops down the field and drops it into a bucket. The first team to get all their socks in the bucket wins.

Tackshop race
Here each member of the team has to pick up an item of tack or grooming equipment, gallop down the field and drop them into a box held by another member.

Five-mug race
The first rider in each team gallops halfway down the field, picks up a mug from a stack upturned on a post, then gallops down the rest of the field to put the mug on top of another post. They then gallop back to the start, and when they get there the second rider sets off. The first team to move all the cups from the first post to the second wins.

Tyre race
In this race a pair of riders race down the field. One jumps off while the other holds her pony, climbs through a tyre, then remounts and the pair gallop back to the start. The first rider dismounts and a third takes her place, and the pair gallop off again and the new rider climbs through the tyre. This goes on until everyone has had a turn and the team to finish first wins.

Stepping stones
In this race, riders have to vault off their ponies, run along a row of upturned buckets, then vault back on again and gallop back to the start.

Glossary

Bit A metal bar that goes in the pony's mouth. It is part of the bridle.

Collected walk A slow walk with short steps. It is used during dressage.

Cross-tied When a pony is tied up in a horsebox or trailer with a rope on each side so it cannot turn round.

Dressage A competition in which a horse or pony has to carry out precise actions and paces.

Fetlocks The lowest joints in a horse's or pony's legs, just above the hooves.

Horsebox A lorry in which horses or ponies are transported.

Lungeing To exercise a horse or pony on a long rein that is attached to a special headcollar. It may or may not be ridden at the same time.

Tack The saddle, bridle and other equipment used on a pony when it is being ridden.

Trailer A type of wagon in which a horse or pony travels. It is towed by a car.

Travel boots Protective pads that cover the lower legs to prevent injury when travelling.

Index

Notes for parents and teachers

Belonging to a branch of The Pony Club or to a local riding club teaches children a lot about ponies and riding that they probably would never learn otherwise, especially if their pony is kept at livery, or if they ride a riding-school pony. They can find out the answers to all kinds of questions, from pony care to problem solving, and have tuition in all aspects of riding. It's also an opportunity to make new friends and have fun.

Different branches of The Pony Club in Britain vary regarding the age at which members can go away to camp. Some allow parents to accompany younger children.

As far as possible, children will have to look after their ponies themselves at Pony Club camp. This will give them a real insight into what caring for ponies is all about. They also have to help with all the domestic chores around the camp.

A child does not have to own a pony to belong to a riding club. Some clubs hold meetings at riding schools, so members without ponies of their own can ride the school's ponies. This can be almost as good as having your own pony, as the child will learn how to look after it, and how to relate to it, as well as how to ride it.

Horse and pony websites

www.pcuk.org
The Pony Club

www.bhs.org.uk
British Horse Society

www.newrider.com
Advice and information for new riders

horseworlddata.com
General information about horses and ponies